C000044596

DOUBLE BINARY

PREVIOUS BOOKS BY RUTH O'CALLAGHAN

Poetry
A Rickle of Bones, Shoestring Press
Unportioned, Salmon
Wringing Blood, Salmon
Mapping the Light, Shoestring Press
An Unfinished Sufficiency, Salmon
Vortices, Shoestring Press
Another Morning of Quiet Pleasures, Soaring Penguin
The Silence Unheard, Shoestring Press
Goater's Alley, Shoestring Press
A Lope of Time, Shoestring Press
Where Acid Has Etched, bluechrome

Echoes From The Steppe: An Anthology of Mongolian Women Poets,
Soaring Penguin

*Without Skin: Interviews with 23 Internationally Renowned Women
Poets*, Soaring Penguin

DOUBLE BINARY

RUTH O'CALLAGHAN

Shoestring Press

All rights reserved. No part of this work covered by the copyright herein may be reproduced or used in any means – graphic, electronic, or mechanical, including copying, recording, taping, or information storage and retrieval systems – without written permission of the publisher.

Printed by imprintdigital
Upton Pyne, Exeter
www.digital.imprint.co.uk

Typesetting and cover design by The Book Typesetters
us@thebooktypesetters.com
07422 598 168
www.thebooktypesetters.com

Published by Shoestring Press
19 Devonshire Avenue, Beeston, Nottingham, NG9 1BS
(0115) 925 1827
www.shoestringpress.co.uk

First published 2022
© Copyright: Ruth O'Callaghan
© Cover photograph: Clare Brant

The moral right of the author has been asserted.

ISBN 978-1-915553-06-5

For Christine

Without whose love and encouragement
this book would never have happened

CONTENTS

Trees   1
Codicil   3

MINDSET
Mindset — 1   7
11   8
She — 1   9
111   10
1V   11
She — 2   12
V   13
She — 3   14
V1   15
She — 4   16
She — 5   17
V11   18
She — 6   19
V111   20

DOUBLE BINARY
Prologue   25
Epilogue   61

MINDSET – HE
Consider   67
Abnegation   68
For Him on the 9.53 out of Clapham Junction   69
Magda   70
The Elected   72
Dog with Bone: Rex Democracy   73
Missionary   74

TREES

We are not a *conspiracy of trees*!
Nor are we *a cathedral of trees*.
We are not so common!
No man's hand has hustled us from quarried stone.
How many deaths did vanity harry before completion?

Vanity we leave to your provenance.
Earth's rhythm is our covenant.
We are not held hostage to hindsight
do not try to retrace lost paths nor seek
to redeem irredeemable days.

Winterbrittle we arch long fingers
reach, naked, toward each other
beyond our own trunks' girth.

Promise was there in spring's harrowed
earth yielding shoots shyly waving
waiting for change on a wind that came
dancing buds into sun's light

summer's greening where you played
hid peccadilloes — we will not call them sins —
leaving your spoor that stained low bushes
sprouting our bole. We did not judge

but were puzzled by your constant change
by never knowing who would, next, rasp back
against our bark yet applauded with gaudy glory
when one fistled our leaves in familiarity

flittered gold on heads now greyed
with season's slack the way we are stripped to black.

*****

We are our own tabernacle. You bore witness as such
gathering beneath us — your insomniac days
endlessly seeking enhancement.

We have known amputation:
chainsaw's body-bite cannot eradicate our presence:
our roots writhe underground, a cursive script
that dismantles boundaries, reaches out
mingles sap, allows our journey to continue.

Such is our persecution, our resurrection —
....and yours?

CODICIL

Trailing absolutions
escapades excused as measure of youth's excess
— we too were once young at time's beginning
offered knowledge to a grasping palm —
yet dark masses behind
hallowed ground is not to be recovered
by shallow promise: desire, dulled, may ripen
unwarmed, even as distant mist curls cold earth.

Time elides:
minute or minuet
both glide past, small steps
you cannot arrest
reversal — lasrever —
impossible.

Mindset

MINDSET — 1

What will we learn from this landscape?
The park gates shut, the promise
of trees and deathless skies

imprisoned within fashioned
wrought iron. Bars guard beds
where complacent tulips colour earth

extract succour from the croci's demise
the ornamental iris shrivelled
snowdrops that fail to show.

Captive outside the walls
we trail the perimeter hunched
grey under the bitter light of security

to spite the day. We are lepers who seek
the intimate inner. Do not offer other
vistas, hills sweeping to sea etc.

they expose us
to unfocused abstractions.
We are indifferent. Resolved. Absolute.

11

There was always the looseness of days
recalcitrant hours, a drought when distraction
was neither sought nor offered, when days folded

each into each, when widows words, layered within
widows weeds, remain in mussel-tight mouths.
A rope of silence holds fast the future

while talk tethers them, beats back
the poverty of lives lost, retrieves longing
for rasp of tongue, chidings, those old arguments

forgotten until, until....
                              Once again, plump as summer
the ease of death wingbeats against a window
under the eaves of this thin house.

A bird flickers, its clear note
accosts the man, name unknown, pain-frail
who lays in abeyance while an inconstant light hovers.

SHE — 1

the kite is   flying
the raven   ravenous
what poor thing   can she do?

111

In a shiver of uncertainty, of unknowing
where symmetry lies fretful and each
interlope of dusk, that larceny of light,
casts a truth for which we are unprepared,

we remain undefined. In the addled dark
the house merges with the hill, a raddle
of leaves ease the dulled election of sky.
A canticle from an unseen bird denotes

despair, sutures the edge of pain, arrests
the air where, penitent, we excise distress,
exclaim this our most precious possession
when only shadow lightens the impending day.

1V

And here is the grief.
Here in this small house
in this small square where

light fleets each window
where absence is exalted
and songs of unseen birds

reside in untended trees

SHE — 2

She contemplates what she will invent
to tincture today's barren hours. So far
she has exercised a lithe body, refined
each *grip, twist, stretch, throw* & *let go*
to extend sinews in accordance with
a TV guru's demands but doesn't think
such exertion has benefitted the kitten.

Yesterday, she practised her knowledge
gained on holiday to Ecuador regarding
guinea pigs but the firm press of nostril
did not elicit the merest wriggle or snuffle
— simply a quiet heaviness in her hand.
She regards the mouse, its litter of paper,
lights a cigarette: this will be her tinder day.

V

The house merges with the hill, interior/
exterior are synonymous, interwoven
truths emerge, proclaim exclusion
dissolution of all we've known

beyond the song of meeting.
Riven, hope transcribes action
interprets what is into what we will
while elision dictates different rhythms

diffuses days, lending fluency to each
nuance. Other voices scuff surfaces
but, beyond all belief, the hush
of an unseen bird admits trust.

SHE — 3

Hours gather in a corner, swarm
over wallpaper, cover camellias
someone — some unseen one —

had printed to gladden drear days.
Now, as she watches, they darken,
seep brown. She admits negligence:

leaves, untended, his fallen blooms,
would have trodden them underfoot.
But these camellias, head-height,

smother, matt hair. Her brush
shushes a bud whose promise
is yet to flower. She cannot allow

propagation: grasps the cold shaft
of her steel comb, folds hands over
the infected area, holds breath. Pierces.

V1

In this space let us deliberate
on the distraction of absence
on how the unsaid cements

the moment, how abstraction
from each casual utterance
renders those few words

potent, renders action impotent:
do not seek solace, rather try
to catch the wind in a net.

SHE — 4

When she walked, the hills gave her direction.
The north/south of her ungoverned thoughts
ignored the sun's contention of east/west

alliance. Pursuit of the sacramental
without collusion of church, murk of incense,
vestments, the priest's shrunk-conker cheeks

led her to where the Word lay, on the page
smeared, smudged, obliterated
by happenstance yet living.

When she sat she thought logic
resounded, yet still there remained
that other life, veracity beyond argument.

SHE — 5

Stitching silences she prays for a return
to labyrinthine days when his curl of kiss
or lip, a cartouche to inscribe upon a body

weary of this now-narrow place, lent each
remark a nuance, a feint blow chosen
to mark disposal of hope, of tedium.

Today her mind consumes anodyne
TV advertisements, drab feathers wilting
this plumage of hours. She yearns for silver

-grey of tern, its territorial slurred burry, beak
thin as a longshoreman's whistle but listens
for his final rale of lung: indifferent

V11

Loss is not absence but transformation.
In absentia a part will become the whole.
No longer a component its completeness
fills each moment with its absent presence.

Deprived, we drive hope forward, reach back
to that time we can never attain to re-visit grief
the way waves wash over sand: a liminal space
where the pulse of pain lives and we can breathe.

SHE — 6

The inarticulate day, for what is there to say
when no words break the air, where nothing
moves beyond boundary of house or garden.

Alarmed, her eyes admit first grudge of light,
squint to curtained windows. Blindly her bare
feet shuffle slippers over soft-comfort-carpet

to parquet-kitchen-cold where the kettle lies
in wait prepared to water a first of many teas
or perhaps a mid-morning coffee just to ring

the changes with a biscuit (or three) before
her ever-earlier lunches to linger with a glass
(or more) of Pinot-Grigio before drowsing down:

fatigue-siestas, the R.4 play ignored, drowned
in not-so-soft snores rising to the goose-honk
that snortles her awake. She is in time to see

the slow lowering of the sun — that glorious
hour in which to first finish the Pinot before
sampling the Burgundy (think ring/changes)

watching pre-viral soaps - even the *Queen Vic.*
is subject to social distancing - but ensures one
more day will be locked-down, hammered to rest.

V111

Uncertain, all being other in these other times
unravelled filaments precipitate shift, diminish
margins in that place between light and dark.

Wind sheathes the trees, stitches fronds of low
growing sallows that sway in unison, laces light
through sturdier branches sheltering a descant

of birds: liturgical. There is no reprise. Unmoored
we hesitate knowing we can only wait while time
that abstract of all abstracts, decodes: concludes.

Double Binary

There are many dimensions to morality.
Adherence to one code may lead
to greater transgression.

What we observe is not nature itself, but nature exposed to our method of questioning.

Werner Heisenberg, 1963

I believe that truth has only one face: that of a violent contradiction.

Georges Bataille

We cannot expect to do anything that is absolutely right. We can only measure rightness by the truth within ourselves. And our own truth will never be quite the same as somebody else's.

Jay Woodman, SPAN

PROLOGUE

Afterwards

One who came holding only their memory
to hang in a closet of oak, who would not
cling to the slightest sapling lest, leafless,
it break beneath weight grave as thought,
lay, still, in dappled light, fingers splayed,
the way a child fends in nightmare-sleep.

This bloody nut's not moving. 'N that jack's bent.
Fuckin' rust bucket! All that rotten judge's fault.
Did he listen? Hell as like. Not one ruddy word!
Gagging for his bloody fodder. Me first offence!
He gets fed I get a four stretch! Business bust.
Me motor reclaimed 'n I'm stuck with this tin can.
Takes me time. Best get rid but…engine's sweet.
'N gotta have wheels. *If* you c'n call this *wheels*.
Rubber down to rim. Second this soddin' week.
How'd he reckon I'm gonna start up on the out?
I ain't goin' on no dole, no *benefits*. Lock 'em up.
Bloody scroungers. Tossers. Ruining the country.
Jus' my bloody luck! I've a man waitin' on a lamb.
A recently lib'rated lamb some fuckin' farmer left
in a field. Prat! But miss the man, miss the money.

Where cliffs crumble dark has not yet fallen
so hope heightens our calling her name.
Early dew clings to gorse-flower, a thin rain,
reluctant to fall, lessens margins between
sea, sky, screens the beach below, cafe
chairs stacked, shackled in chains: waves
caress the bay, the sand pale as her face.

Nettles — hairs hollow, hypodermic, toxic —
on leaf, stem, refute every man's grasp,
reveal subspecies each equally dangerous,
reveal small-bird bones, gulls scavenging,
rapacious: such predators, opportunistic,
display guile, defeat even closest guard:
control those accidents of time or place.

I called and called my voice ever-higher, falsetto
a candidate for a cappella or the local choir
I called until I was a broken string.

So I'm on me knees in all this shit. Bastard judge!
No way was it like they say. She loved it. Laughed.
Her teeth were perfect white. So bright! 'N a gap.
I held her hands in her lap. In mine. She shook but
looked into me eyes all the time. Felt me fingers
trippin' round but didn't cry out. Well. Only once.
Fingers…dipped. Penetrated. Could've bin worse!
It weren't John Thomas. I couldn't bloody help it!
Honest. It was that gap. 'N me tongue there…
an' elsewhere. So….me concentration slipped.
Bit too hasty….Like that bloody judge 'n his food.
'S me who paid. Still payin'….Bugger Insurance.
Tax. Jus' keep to the backs. Pull into side. Wave.
Changed man? No way! But I'm a man changing
a wheel cos of some deranged judge. All *his* *f*ault.

She sought Narnia-land behind frocks, fake furs
in Nana's wardrobe, led many lives, began, *would,*
only answer to *her* chosen name, Alice, did not seek
to slaughter Giant Grump but teach him meekness,
to love small animals whom she rescued on a daily
or even hourly basis: a cat from a sack, a dog tied
in a dirt yard: she cried when a web held fast the fly.

She loved all weathers, all seasons, would skip in snow,
finger pearls of rain running round the brim of her hat.
She woke into a hurry of day, scampered through fields,
over stiles, dry walls, leapt long-legged over bumps,
laughing *Tumps, Mr. Mole* but crept under mile-high sky
to stroke a velvet crab, his short coat of hairs, unafraid
of its red eyes, feisty pincers: other name, devil crab.

I hear my voice crack.
I wait, still. So still. Waiting for a shrill
Father — if in Alice mode — or dad if my Alex..

Betcha I've bloody busta gut with that ruddy nut....
So I let her leg it. After. But fuck-judge ignored that.
Looked at me like I'm a lump of turd under his boot.
Fair trial? No way. I knew she'd say but I'd be gone
'fore she were home. Weren't known in those parts
so weren't bothered. Felt...elated. Smelt her again
when a sodding speed cop.... Five fuck miles over!
Billboards brag 'bout all them they stop. Can't bang
every bugger up so got a caution. Didn't cotton on
what'd occurred. But he clocked me details. Plates.
Make. Van. White. Jeans greasy. Dead give away....
They hinted leniency if kid di'n't have go to court
Cop reckoned a rat. Knew *Something amiss.* Piss off!
Ponce! It so weren't me fingers. Wiped 'em on grass.
Four stretch! Betcha judge kept a poker up his arse.

At an alteration of light, an intimation of mist,
we will turn from the distant stream of beach,
we will turn toward our rented fairy-tale cottage
where thatch sweeps down flushed-pink walls,
where geraniums weep blood on white stucco,
where unripe apricots hang, their short season
never bearing fruition but pleasing to the eye.

Her hair fell over her eyes as she undressed
ivy from the balcony, the glossy leaves curled,
garlanded her young fingers as it had crowned
ancient heads, poets, athletes, intellectuals,
wearing prevents drunkenness — Bacchus
bears witness — indicates fidelity, protects
against all evil. How will Alice bear witness?

I changed tone. Went from stern-commanding to bully-boy shout, demanding to a gentle p-l-e-a-s-e, terminating in a moan.

Mum visited. Once. Hair all bleach 'n frizz. Usual.
Said, she'll be bloody bald. Didn't listen. Didn't stop.
Just long enough to mention never to come back.
Charmin'. Had some feller parked…. He'll be a D.
he's had 'em all. *I've* had 'em all. *Uncles*. Uncle Del.
Uncle Den. Uncle Dave. Uncle Don. It goes on. 'N on.
Said she had a *penchant* for fellers beginnin' with D.
Trouble was, they had a *penchant* for me. Ev'ry night.
School called her in 'cos I was fallin' asleep. *Don't
mention the uncles. You'll be locked away. Well away.*
Thought 'bout it but knew they'd have *uncles* there.
Think I was seven. Six? Dunno. Old enough to know
hers'd leave. Eventually. Another poor bugger's turn….
'S a circle….I was eleven when Dimitri came. Foreign.
Took me to the fair. 'N I thought. *Here we go again.*

I should never have agreed but he'd bought wine,
laid a rug, inveigled me into a monastery of trees
Sunday steepled above us. We splayed there, free,
the cool nectar glowing yellow. And he was a god,
his face shining above mine, his fine-fingered hand
lacing mine or roving toward secret, forgotten places.
We had never been so close since…since Alice….

....since Alice overrode Alex.
I tried to buy a 10 minute Alice-free
New-Age-free world: discover pre-child wild!

But never had a foreigner. Diff'rent. 'N he was diff'rent.
Didn't want me to….'N didn't touch. Jus' held me hand
on the Wall of Death. Pretended *he* was scared, not me.
'N he saw my face when I saw *her* riding the carousel.
She's on one of 'em painted horses rising high. Smiling.
She had this hair. Red. Red as sun. Blazin' sun. Burnin'.
The higher the horse rode the wider her smile. At me.
'N I felt all funny down….you know… Dimitri knew too.
Took me for a burger. Sat in a quiet corner. 'Xplained.
'S okay. She's a girl. 'S natural….in me pants. Took me
back to the ride….We spent all night lookin' round fair.
She weren't there. I welled up. Dim put his arm around.
He'd been so kind so I…I….He hit me. *Nefer wif man!*
Girl all time. Old. Young. All very fine. Man. Burn in hell!
Make mistake, make away. Destroy. Make reparation.

Before we married he could be so persuasive.
Although he did not understand the Alpha state,
I would take his hand, lay it against my breast,
perform puja, to allow our auras to embrace.
He would encircle me. Slowly. His face so alive!
I knew he would be receptive, eventually, so now
I thought this would be the time to reminisce, to ....

….but no! The nagging began again: Alice!
You may wish to live your life based on fallacy
somehow some of us survive in reality. He is Alex!

Filth came. 5 a.m. Dim's illegal. Cuffed him. No need.
I make mistake. Make reparation. Remember always.
Then he weren't there. So I searched the fair alone.
Days. Nights. Nobody never smiled like that. Not ever.
Not at me....Laters, did dates....One girl's mate said
she's on a dare. So stopped. School. Dates. Hung 'bout.
Park. Mall. Met a kid cryin'. I bent. She nooses me neck
with her arms so I held her underneath. Take the weight.
It felt so good...jus' to hold. Jus' normal like a...a father.
Jus' walkin' with me arms around. 'N she smiled. At me!
Then a madhag starts screamin' in me face. Didn't listen.
The crowd jumped me. Filth came an' I ...I...I shit meself.
Filth didn't wanna know. Took me home. Empty. As usual.
Weren't gonna hurt the kid....It jus'... jus' felt...so good....
Dim! That shit?...Make mistake 'n me body gave way?

The earth depressed as he climbed, limbs heavy, feral,
hands pawing my body, my glass knocked from grasp.
I saw the grass shrivel. Abusive, he refuses to recognise
anima in his child. I hoped if I closed my eyes, a half-smile
on my lips he'd see I needed repose, accept that we must
trust inner innocence. Vigilance is required, not mockery.
Why must she commit: wear trousers but not a frock?

It's sheer bloody crazy for you to encourage him.
It's merely a phase. I don't disparage him!
There's other ways! Footie, boxing....

Dim would've understood. Could've told 'em how it was but those bastards'd locked him away. I jus' stood there. Di'n't know whatta say. Then *mother* turns up 'n for once di'n't stink of that cheap drink used on the littly's. Sweet. As shit....She used her charm. Sez I di'n't mean no harm. Loved kids like her. 'Cept I wouldn't abuse 'em like her. Not then. Me head was still full of the girl on the carousel. Dreamt if we went together we'd have our own. Never felt like that 'bout those slags from school. That kid in the mall ...could've been ours.... Should've. 'Cept for mousey hair. Fuckbutt said that was *A prior incident*. No way! She weren't burnin' sun red! Not like the one I got done for. I'm not bent! I got sent down 'cos fuckbutt wanted lunchI Di'n't listen! I jus' meant a tickle but when she smiled I closed me eyes 'n...was...like...transported...back to that fair. She was.....

But he couldn't let matters lie. He couldn't let me lie
bathed in sunlight, mother earth beneath my body,
pulsing my seven centres, my core, my astral body,
urgent to bilocate. I heard the cry — *Alice, Alice* —
yet he kept prodding the way one prods a rock pool,
wary of what may be hidden in subterranean depths.
Prod. Prod. Prod. Prod! I am not a crustacean!

YOU HAVE MURDERED MY SON!

…straddlin' her horse, risin' 'n dippin' an' her smilin'. AT ME!
Put out me hand 'n coulda touched her leg. Tickled her leg.
So when this one with her red hair smiled that's what I did.
'S all I did…till I closed me eyes. It was all the horse's fault.
Goin' up 'n down. Higher and higher an' me hand followed.
I weren't lookin'. I di'n't know what it was doin'! It moved….
By itself. Me eyes were closed tight so no way could I see
what it was doin'….Till she wriggled. 'N then ! opened 'em.
She were lookin' right at me 'n I figured she'd been doin' it
all along. Then she smiled…or cried… or summat 'n I saw
that gap 'n I was back. At the fair…'N I…'N I cum…'N Dim
was whisperin' in me ear *'S all right. She a girl. But no hurt.*
No hurt. Let her go. Let her go. Could hear him clear as day.
So okay. Let her leg it….No way did anyone know me there.
…Then I got busted by that bloody clever cop. Four years!

I heard the rhythms thrashing the earth, earth's force
moving surely upon its own path, nascent, moving
to where the improbable becomes possible, moving
ineluctably toward where the unknown's inescapable:
knew I must return, must remove myself, lose myself
in its throb, drag my body from under his grunt-voice,
his constant demands for proof, disregard for choice.

He's less than eleven!
For heaven's sake, Jake's scared.
Wary. Is it Alice or Alex coming to his comp.?

For Jake's sake, listen! He has exams. next year.
He's told you of his fear — Alex will be bullied.
Jake will be busy and a necklace of stone

won't protect nor having a mother who hugs a tree.
Why can't you see? Jake will suffer their malice
having a brother who calls himself Alice,

Cop's fault. That flamin' sentence. Him 'n fuckbutt.
Fair? Justice? Jesus! I weren't no pretty boy. Defo.
They still shafted me. 'N fer afters? A shit sandwich.
Like I'm one o' them pervs. Homos. In the communal.
Don't drop the soap. Ain't no joke. 'S all nuts 'n butts.
Pig-screws turn a blind one. Complain 'n get grundies
shoved down yer throat…or it's slit. That or yuh balls.
Then you'll sing high. So? Stay on the wing? Go solo?
…No way. Not gonna thank some bastard for grub
he's wanked over. Smilin'….Do Paedo Palace? Nah
Like Dim says, *Make mistake. Make away. Reparation.*
Bloody psyches reckon you're in for their recreation.
Admit you're a nonce. Sign up for *treatment.* My arse.
Refuse 'n you could be up for an indeterminate. Nonce.
          Not On Normal Communal Exercise.

He dismisses our ways, favours only what is proven.
The necklace was a gift from a Shaman who taught me
what is known is not always present and what is present
is not always known. I have been shown other paths,
other worlds, given prescience: his shallow adherence
to fingering untruths of familiar, tired gods will be riven.
Alice and I will evolve onto the causal plane. Nirvana!

His hair is too long.
You dyed it too blonde.
Why not spike it — retro punk?

Pay back time? Them self-styled, so-called hard men
normal? 'S joke. 'S jus' an excuse to go with a bloke.
They keep it well hid. So reckon I done 'em a favour
going with a kid. The sod lot o' 'em's pervy.. Burn in hell.
Them. Not me. They forced me. I've only gone with girls.
Dim said 's'kay if they're young jus' not to go all the way,
fingers, tongue…but never with a feller. He was with me.
In there. Not in the flesh see. They'd shipped him out.
Dunno where. Dunno where Dim come from. I were lonely.
Not chattin' with nonces! Or bum boys. So I talked to him.
'S only way not to go crazy. He kept me straight. Listened.
I was grateful. Took his advice. Di'n't tell that sick psych….
Not on me release chat….

        Fuck! Whassat?…Van's rockin'.
Kids foolin'…? I'll crack their bloody….Christ! Just one kid.
A girl. Climbin' in. By herself. She's after the bloody lamb!

Now I see time tumble-weeding down the street. A warning!
Alice is bound within its wheel. Knots hold her. A new epoch
is evolving. I can feel her pain, smell fragrance from her T.
That beautiful T! Sequins emblazoned her proud philosophy.

All Girls Can

He commands me to refuse what he deems *His son's demands*
but he resists the existence of distant Nirvana, denies our child's
true nature, our true daughter, so it is my duty to dismiss him.

You think you're more sensitive than me but I begged you
not to buy that T. Sound-bite-sequins are trite
and I have a right to state He is not a girl!

If your tumbling time is an omen and not
simply artifice, we'd best call the police. Smartish.
You started this, you phone, I'll do the rest: kettle, tea!

Oi! You! You tryin' to nick me sheep?....Don' give me no cheek.
Not if you don' wanna come to no harm. Coulda busted me arm!
Cos of you bloody jack slips.....Swearing? Lippy little bugger!
Your parents should be 'shamed lettin' you run wild out o' school.
If you were my child....I know it's a lamb...Holiday? Nice one!
From London! Why you cry...?...I ain't taking it for no slaughter.
....Buy?....You got money then? Thought so. Brassic....Don' cry!
Spoil that lovely T. Wassit say?....Can what?...Can be tickled.
I'll tickle yuh with yuh pretty hair. Betcha I c'n getcha to laugh....
There....Look. D'yuh wanna come 'n meet the man whose gonna
take care of the lamb. That way you know he's okay. Watcha say?
Yeah? I'll drop yuh afters....'Course you c'n hold it but stay in back.
Way too dodgy in front. Can't risk cops pulling me over, can we?
Hold him tight. Lamb's c'n be frisky....Nah. Ain't none in me van.
Water's at the man's. 'S'at okay?...Right. I'll jus' slam the shutter.

A falter of light, a cry of crow skims slant tiles
mounting the porch beyond which the 'phone,
cream, lies idle in its cradle awaiting touch, waiting
to be picked up, held, before impact, keys punched
to bring life into wires streaming continuous current
above mile upon mile upon mile of wet-dark tarmac
Emergency. Which service do you require?

Under the neutral burr of his voice I hear bells of fuschia
whisper, colluding with the wires, with the white apricots
that drop unripe fruit on an untended lawn: my child
was untended as we slipped away for one glass of wine,
now light is slipping from the garden where my absent child
played today. Steam weeps the windows. The voice persists:
Emergency. Which service do you require?

Only one: my child home safely. To all other,
whether my wife, his odd mother,
I'm indifferent. I have no need.

It weren't my fault! It was jus' gonna be a tickle. 'N a little fiddle.
She's holdin' the lamb close 'n I was strokin' it 'n strokin' her T.
Jokin'. *All Girls Can*….I sez, *Can't. Can't drive a van.* She sez,
It's my philosophy. Proper grown up like. The lamb wriggled.
Skipped away. I teased her *Girls can't even keep hold a lamb.*
Went on her knees crawling after 'n I saw her thigh 'n me hand
…reached out 'n she stayed still 'n me hand jus' moved higher
…'n higher like it had a will of its own. It slipped me finger inta
her knickers 'n made me voice sing…. *It wiggled, 'n wiggled
'n wiggled inside her.*…I di'n't have no choice cos down in me…
Wett'r'n time I saw red head on the carousel 'n I was…elated.
That hand! It ripped her knickers, forced me head down…
Made me…taste her. Made me hard. So hard…till I touched…
She weren't no girl 'n I would burn in hell. 'N Dim sez, *Make away.*
Make mistake, make away. So I…I k…I kil… I… *I made reparation.*

Emergency. Which service do you require?

EPILOGUE

I heard aprons of rain sweep the garden,
a clamour heavy against the storm door we,
careless, left open: sirens on the trunk road
sullied the dusk. A white van's wheels over
that same wet-dark tarmac devours distance,
grinds towards woods, disturbs rank grass.
I pray to Cosmos to keep the Keres at bay.

I came to hate Judas hope.
That startle toward
an unknown girl.

She turns. Face blank.
I back away, my apologies
spill from dry lips: I need a drink.

I see his pain but cannot reach out to heal his spirit.
He chases unreal dreams of a child restored. Refuses
to come to terms with what these earthly authorities
have found: at least foxes had not disturbed her mound.
He refuses to see what follows death is not dissolution
but evolution! *Our* evolution will be our dissolution —
divorce! But it is incumbent on me, Cosmos decrees....

People in shops stop talking.
Trolleys create a swathe between
me and them. Fear hugs their child close.

Leprosy is contagious. Suspicious eyes glint.
A boy? girl? disappeared? You must know
something not told. Yes. I need a drink!

....to help him not to sink into despair, to reach for beer, rum.
I cannot bring him to care for those spheres which comfort me
— Nirvana, Devachen — Heaven to him. I have progressed,
he has regressed, rejects my teas possess special properties,
mocks their names: Beings of Light, Devil Slayer, Earth Apple,
Moon Medicine, Heart of the Forest, Wounded Healer.
Each cup is placed facing its pre-destined direction but he....

I snatch a can from the ice-box.
The ring-pull resists. I twist its neck.
Tear back: hear her sobs wreathe the air.

I need a pig's ear. Bloody pull breaks.
That T. led me on. Sending a message.
Like Dim said, *Girl all time. Old. Young....*

A crucifixion of aerials scar the darkening sky,
a tern, returning home, pauses,
beak dripping silver saliva.

The moon silvers her coverlet: her Greeter
ensures clearing has been achieved. Free
from earth's gravitational pull her life will be
unrestricted by space or time: transitional!
Yet a silver cord links our kindred souls, will,
I hope, delay her entering a higher state until
I arrive: we will enter Summerland together!

Jake sat A-Level Art.
Subject: Still Life. Asked:
Can you scrub blood from grass?

Mindset – HE

CONSIDER

Nota Bene
>   the schoolyard where a child cleaves
against the wall, back guarded as he trembles
on the edge of shadow where others play: unregarded.
Relief comes in the summon of bell,
of desk-internment, of interrogation on theorem,
Pythagorean, by Mr. Copage, erratic and short

of temper, who fails to
>   consider the ravine the boy
has failed to broach, who notes only his correct
text-book answers and marks him both for life
and Oxbridge, *his* Alma Mater where, trembling
against a buttress, he watched students swarm
arm in arm across the quad, knew such warmth

was not for him to
>   consider *now* but to regard only
in the future and then to the degree, he smiles
at his silent pun, they influence his career — fails
to wrest it from regret. He trembles back against
the blackboard knowing he can never retrieve
unmapped friendships where play marked lives.

ABNEGATION

He once saw a boat, feared
it too far to swim though near
enough to observe the man,
his line steady in clear water,
hat brim held slant, covering
against the all-too-bright sun,
absorbed in pursuing small
fish that stipple the surface,
while bigger that rise beside
his bait dive again, leaving
only a shadow, leaving him.

FOR HIM ON THE 9.53 OUT OF CLAPHAM JUNCTION

All that remains of this particular porker is a shred
dangling from the beard of one so wedded to grasp
the last lone bacon roll from under my outstretched
hand that he will wield elbows more lethal than any
mere stun gun employed to kill the pig, so causing
consternation to Katya who's travelled all the way
from Latvia for the privilege of serving Middle White,
an endangered species engendered, it is rumoured,
by a cross with the Cumberland now extinct, but which,
according to Wikipedia, retains distinctive pricked ears,
enabling him to detect possible movement towards
fodder on which he, determined to possess, snaffles
into his short snout before a less-endowed fellow,
who can only snort in despair at being robbed by this
re-incarnation of a crossed Cumberland, before he
remembers how, in the old days, raising a hatchet
to be brought down with murderous intent, ensures
a skittery chase that many say creates a crisp skin
when the pig is finally consigned to the spit; such
scenarios are less likely now with mechanisation
although the old ways are still said to be chosen
on the Pannonian Plain; in particular, in the region
of the Carpathian Basin, the vogue is to butchering
in such a manner, the pig being vague in areas
of social niceties which brings me to the matter
of him on the 9.53 and the dead fly in the corner.

I know nothing of the dead fly in the corner but…

MAGDA

He slouches there, his voice gross with righteousness,
an occasional pulse shifts in his neck behind the blubber
of chins resting on a barrel chest keeping its thin grey
hair from the dark coarseness snaking from his nose.

He'd brought her from the Eastern bloc. Refusal to specify
a country gave rise to speculation in the village, pop.1,343.
Her guttural sounds shied children to hug behind fathers' legs,
having heard the word 'invasion' intoned from the war before.

We saw her just after dawn skittering the hill for the paper
he'd peruse while she fried his eggs, bacon, black pudding,
before the flee down again for 7a.m. shift, skirts flapping,
undone — and we knew he'd been at his old ways again.

The day the factory belt broke down she stayed late, knew
no other way but to do as ordered by authority. Coming from *there*
did not expect extra pay so he suffered from being no wealthier
for his dinner being delayed. She fasted: feasted her eyes

on his tiny incisors gnawing each shred of meat from the bone
before a fling into an open sack drunk with rubbish. We learnt later
she retrieved them, sucked their whiteness silently once his snores
covered creak of bare boards, the clink of glass as she drained

dregs from bottles *he'd* swigged during the day.
                                    No one knows when
she went or where. Just that her place on the belt was empty
                                            one day
and him roaring like a bull not able to mount a cow. It took
                                            two days
before we realised Donny, the village fool, no longer lounged
                                            outside

the factory by the war memorial. That same memorial that *he*
had erected,
begrudgingly, to distract villagers dwelling on the first wife's
scandal.

THE ELECTED

Angled behind the podium, face averted, you unravelled
each and every argument, posited false philosophy,
substantiated improbable propositions, encouraged us
to swallow wholesale the new order, segue from false
premise to foregone conclusion.

                            Steeped in misery
we laughed: indolence lay ahead, diligence behind.

DOG WITH BONE: REX DEMOCRACY

Rex. I'm going to throw out your bone, said the bone-throwing
owner.
One last gnaw before I toss it, master? pleaded the bone-
throwing dog.
What about me! Do I not have a say? said the dog-thrown
bone.

MISSIONARY

McCready, laying down his pick-axe, declared it behove
an Irish gentleman and scholar such as himself to propagate
– a word learnt in literacy classes – knowledge and, to avail
himself of the wherewithal to do so. he's prepared to travel
to the farthest flung corners of the earth without the fear
of scabies, rabies, pygmies, elephantiasis or dementia –
this from the man who lay whimpering in the bath at the sight
of a daddy long legs. Attempts to dissuade him with the mention
of monsoons, typhoons, Parsees, Pharisees and the odd tsunami,
only persuaded him to treat us to a dismissive diatribe regarding
the biblical forty days and forty nights of rain which any true
Kerry man calls summer. When we deemed his donkey jacket
insufficient for all occasions – at the very least a pith helmet
was a necessary addition to his sartorial elegance – he flourished
his latest purchase from Oxfam, complete with miner's lamp.
On being informed slithering creatures of the damp demanded
the donning of gaiters he gloated, now being *au fait* with —
through *The Learned Irish Roadmender's Guide to Africa* —
the fourth lower tooth of both 'gator and croc, the notch of
                                                    the latter
leaving it visible with the closing of the mouth but dental
                                                    inspection
was not pre-eminent in his intentions. Neither was a visit to
                                                    Antarctica,
knowing that far south cold could loosen the gold tooth in *his*
                                                    mouth
and, truth to tell, what was Iceberg Alley except an omission
                                                    of God
to defrost? Perhaps Alaska would prove similar for he'd heard
                                                    a man
on the tube talking about the inside passage which was
                                                    downright rude
in front of ladies, medical conditions involving itches being
                                                    confined
to consultations with the quack when you wanted the note
                                                    signed off

to go back to the old country, thirsting for a glass of the black
                                                              stuff
straight from the draught. Weary of educating the English who
                                                              spoke
not a word of Irish, McCready slings his pick over his
                                                              shoulder,
declares he'll begin his safari in sunny Ballygally and boldly
                                                              follow
to where the wistful wind sings softly to the Ballaboura
                                                              Mountains.